Great Men of Science

# HAROLD UREY

*The Man Who Explored from Earth to Moon*

ALVIN AND VIRGINIA SILVERSTEIN

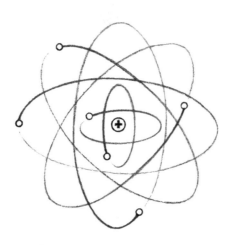

*Illustrated by Lee J. Ames*

71– 93118

THE JOHN DAY COMPANY · NEW YORK

*For Harold and Frieda Urey*

# Acknowledgment

The authors are deeply grateful to Dr. Harold Urey, without whose patient cooperation and help this book could not have been written.

*The John Day Company, 257 Park Avenue, New York, N.Y. 10010*
*an Intext publisher*

*Published on the same day in Canada by Longmans Canada Limited.*

*Library of Congress Catalogue Card Number: 74-125573*
*Printed in the United States of America*

# Contents

# In the Beginning

It was the earth of long ago. The lands were bleak and barren, and scarred by moonlike craters. Nothing moved except great swirls of dust whipped up by the restless winds and spouts of flaming lava from the mouths of erupting volcanos. Lightning crackled through the air, and huge torrents of rain fell upon the lands and washed down into the seas.

On all the earth there was no life. But the beginnings of life were there. With each crackle of lightning the chemicals of life were forming high in the air above and falling down upon the lands and seas below. Somewhere in the warm seas, the spark of life arose and spread throughout the world. Time and time again old forms of life gave rise to new ones. And as the life forms of the earth changed, the earth itself changed too, until it came more and more to resemble the world we know today.

How do we know that this is the way life began on our planet?

No man was there to watch the story of life unfolding. Scientists have pieced together many different kinds of evidence to work out their theories of how life began on earth. One of the leaders in the field is Harold C. Urey. Indeed, it was his idea that sparked one of the most important experiments on the origin of life. In his laboratory scientists for the first time reproduced the conditions of the ancient earth and found a way that the chemicals of life might have been formed there.

Today this great scientist is examining rocks brought back by astronauts from the moon. He and other scientists are trying to work out the history of the moon and cast some further light on the history of the earth and our solar system as well.

With all these exciting discoveries, it is suprising that Harold Urey won his Nobel Prize for something entirely different, the discovery of a new kind of hydrogen. He has worked in many fields, and his life has been a fascinating one indeed.

# A Country Boyhood

Harold Clayton Urey was born on April 29, 1893, in Walkerton, a small town in Indiana near South Bend. Harold's father, Samuel Clayton Urey, was a schoolteacher, and the family was

Harold Urey at three months of age.

G. D. Ewing

very proud of him. He had been born in a log cabin in a wild part of the country. He had worked hard and managed to get a college degree, which was quite unusual in those days. Now Samuel Urey was determined that his children too would get the best possible education that he could give them.

Young Harold's first memory, from when he was about two years old, was of pressing his nose between the pickets of the fence around the yard and wondering what was on the other side. He never did find out, because the family moved to Glendora, California, before Harold was old enough to go out exploring on his own. But later in life he would find himself wondering about many things. And as he learned how to go about searching for answers, he made a number of discoveries that no one in the world had ever made before.

The years in California were a golden time of tasting sand out of an old spoon and learning to ride a bicycle and sitting in the shade of the green pepper trees. Picking green oranges and piling them up in a neat pile earned young Harold a sound spanking.

Those were happy years for the Ureys. Harold's brother Clarence, just two years younger, was soon old enough to play with him. Then, when Harold was nearly five, a baby sister Martha was born. But the Urey family did not stay in California long.

When Harold was six, Samuel and Cora Urey took their three young children back to Indiana to stay with Grandmother Urey on her farm. The children were too small to realize it, but there was a sad reason for the move. Samuel Urey was very ill with tuberculosis, and he was not able to work any more.

That fall Harold started school in a little country schoolhouse nearby. His father had been teaching him his letters, and now

8

each night the boy proudly read to his father from his school-books. But these quiet days were not to last long either. Later that fall Samuel Urey died.

Harold's mother and grandmother were both widows now, and it was a struggle for them to keep up the farm and take care of the children. But they worked hard to make sure that Harold and his brother and sister would always have enough food to eat and clothes to wear. In many farm families, the children often stayed home from school to help out with the chores. But not the Ureys. Cora Urey saw to it that all three children went to school every day. Sometimes at night she would take out a worn bankbook and smile to herself. Her husband had had an insurance policy, and the money from the policy was to be used for the children's education. At least she had that for the future. No matter how hard things became, she would never spend a penny of it for anything else.

The Urey children missed their father. But there were still many happy times. In the winter they went sliding down the snow-covered hills, to land in a giggling, tumbled heap at the bottom. Sometimes their Grandfather Reinoehl, Cora's father, bundled them up in a warm buffalo robe and took them out for a sleighride.

Every Sunday the Ureys went to church. They were members of the Brethren Church, a pacifist group that sincerely believed that all wars are wrong. In later years Harold would begin to wonder about some of the things he had learned in church, and he gradually developed his own beliefs about God and the world. But he would always remember these early teachings, and he vowed to do whatever he could to try to stop wars.

Some of the farm work was too heavy for women and children, even if they were as willing workers as the Ureys. Grandmother Urey hired a man, Martin Alva Long, to help with the heavy chores. He was strong and quiet and kind, and he got along well with the children. In time Martin Long and Cora Urey grew to love one another, and when Harold was ten they were married. A year later Grandmother Urey died. Martin, Cora, and the children moved to another farm about five miles away, farther into the country.

It was a happy life for the Urey children in their new home. Their stepfather was good to them, and he too always made sure that they would never have to stay out of school, no matter how much work there was to be done on the farm. In the summer, of course, there were plenty of chores to do. They were growing onions for the market, and all day long, week after week, Harold and his brother would work out in the hot summer sun, weeding the onion fields. But there was time for fun, too—walks in the woods and swimming and fishing in nearby Cedar Lake.

Seven months out of the year, school was in session. Each day the Urey children walked a mile and a half to the little country school. It was here that a teacher showed Harold a way of studying that would help him very much in the future. This method was to read each lesson very carefully, understanding each sentence completely before going on to the next one. It was slow studying this way, but after Harold had read his assignment once he really knew it and did not have to go over it again.

When Harold Urey was fourteen, he was graduated from grade school. He had to take an examination given by the State of Indiana in order to graduate. He scored a 76—just one point over the passing grade of 75. It did not look as though Harold was a very bright student, but at least his score was good enough to get him into high school.

Going to high school in Kendallville, Indiana, was a new experience for Harold Urey. He had been raised on a farm and had gone to a small country school with other farm children. Now he was going to school in a big town of five thousand people. He was very shy at first—all the other students seemed so worldly and sophisticated.

Harold quickly overcame his shyness and began to make friends. He joined the debating team and soon found that he enjoyed making speeches. He was so good at it in fact that he even entered an oratorical contest; his speech on Theodore Roosevelt won him a five-dollar gold piece. All the teachers who knew that Harold had barely passed his grade school examinations were amazed to find that he quickly went to the top of his high school class. And all through high school and later in college too, he scored the highest grades in his classes.

In high school Harold studied English and Latin, mathematics and biology and physics, and some political science and history. He found all his subjects so interesting that it was hard to choose which he liked best. He learned John Milton's poem "L'Allegro" by memory and still remembers much of it. But best of all he loved Latin, mainly because his Latin teacher, E. E. Kling, was the most inspiring teacher he had ever met. Harold decided that he too would become a Latin teacher.

# Changing Plans

In 1911, when Harold Urey finished high school, it was much simpler to become a teacher than it is now. All a person had to do was graduate from high school, pass some examinations, and then take about three months of education courses at a college. So at eighteen, after completing his three months at Earlham College in Indiana, Harold was officially a country school teacher.

His first assignment was in a small country school near the County Seat in Albion, Indiana. Harold taught about two dozen children in various grades. After a year at this school, the young teacher decided to go to Montana, to join his family again. For Martin and Cora Long had heard of a new opportunity on a ranch near Big Timber, Montana. And they had taken all the younger children—the other two Ureys and three more little girls who had been born since their marriage—to live on the new ranch.

After joining his family, Harold soon got a job teaching in a small wooden schoolhouse at the foot of the Absarokee Mountain Range. After a year there he transferred to another school across the valley, in a nearby mining camp. While he was at the Absarokee Mountain school, he stayed with the Wilson family, and gradually he came to an important new decision.

For some time Harold had been growing restless and dissatisfied. More and more he was feeling that he did not want to spend the rest of his life as a country schoolteacher. But if he was going to try anything more ambitious, he would need a better education. Then the Wilsons' son Brian decided to go to college. Soon Harold was convinced that this was what he, too, wanted to do. His share of the money from his father's insurance policy had all been used up on his high school education. But he had been working for three years, and although country school teaching did not pay much, he had saved up a small sum. If he could get a part-time job after classes, he could just manage to get along. It was worth a try!

In the fall of 1914, just as World War I was starting in Europe, Harold Urey went to Missoula, Montana, to register at the University of Montana. Since his high school days, his ideas had changed a great deal. He still found Latin interesting and helpful in learning new English words that had originally come from Latin. But he no longer wanted to become a Latin teacher. Now he had decided to major in psychology, to learn more about why people act the way they do. But at the University of Montana he received a surprise—the Psychology Department did not take any freshmen. So he registered for courses in chemistry, biology, English, German, and French; he would take his psychology courses later. He also quickly found the part-time job he needed, waiting on tables in the girls' dormitory.

15

The University of Montana was a small school at the time, with only about five hundred students. Harold soon came to know many of his professors personally, and they had much helpful advice for this serious, bright young student. Harold was carrying an unusually heavy schedule—so heavy that he was able to finish his college work in three years instead of the usual four. And even though he was working part-time besides, he had A's in all his subjects.

Harold Urey was very lucky to meet some fine teachers at the University of Montana, especially in chemistry and biology. One of them, Professor Archibald Bray in biology, had a degree from Cambridge University in England. Professor Bray was a born teacher who was fascinated with his subject and knew

DR. HAROLD C. UREY
NOBEL PEACE PRIZE
IN SCIENCE 1934
TAUGHT HERE 1911

how to spark the same enthusiasm in his students. He organized some of the young men into a discussion group that he called "the authentic society." They spent hours after class talking about many things—not only biology, but also religion and philosophy as well. It was not until many years later that Harold Urey realized that in this small town in Montana, Professor Bray had helped to give him and the other students in the group the same kind of tutorial education that students receive in the expensive private universities in England.

In his studies with Professor Bray and the other teachers at the university, Harold became more and more fascinated with biology. He was particularly interested in the study of microscopic one-celled creatures called protozoa. In his first research project, supervised by Professor Bray, he collected samples of water and mud from a little backwater of the Missoula River and studied the protozoa that it contained. He was amazed and intrigued by the tiny creatures—so small that they could not be seen without a microscope, but still able to live and eat and reproduce themselves. It seemed to him that they must be the simplest forms of life that could exist, perhaps very much like the first creatures that ever lived in the world. Later Urey discovered that these early ideas had been quite wrong—that protozoa are actually very complicated organisms. But his first wonderings about how life really began on earth date back to those quiet afternoons collecting samples on the banks of the Missoula River and peering through his microscope in the laboratory at the strange creatures he had captured.

In his second year at the university, Harold's professors got him a job as an assistant in the Biology Department. With the money he earned from this position, and from a summer spent working on a nearby railroad and an irrigation project, he was

able to finish his college courses by the spring of 1917. By this time he was convinced that he knew what he wanted to do with his life. He loved biology, and he deeply admired the work that his professors were doing at the university. So he had resolved to become a college biology teacher.

But just as Harold Urey felt that he had made up his mind about his career at last, events were occurring in the world that would soon force him to change his plans once again. The war had been going on all through Harold's college years, and now, in the spring of 1917, the United States entered the war. Many of the young men that Harold knew quickly enlisted in the fight. Now he was faced with a difficult decision.

Harold Urey had been raised to believe that war was wrong, and he still sincerely believed this. But somehow he could not help feeling that fighting *this* war was necessary. The German government under the Kaiser was a very stern and rigid government that did not give much freedom to the people. The army was a very strong power in Germany at the time. Harold felt that if it was not stopped soon, it would spread this type of government throughout the world. What could he do?

One of Harold's former chemistry professors, Professor Rhodes, had a solution. He had gone to work with the Barrett Chemical Company in Philadelphia, Pennsylvania. Now he wrote to Harold, telling him how badly chemists were needed to make explosives and other chemicals for the war effort. This seemed to be an answer to Harold's problem. And so he went to Philadelphia to work as a chemist.

The war seemed very far away to Harold as he worked at the Barrett Chemical Company. Of course he watched the headlines anxiously, and he breathed a sigh of relief when his brother, who had been in the army, came home safely. And he grew discouraged to see how quickly new troubles sprang up in the world after the "war to end all wars" was over. But more and more Harold Urey was becoming involved in his work and developing an absorbing interest in chemistry. After the war was over, the need for chemists dropped off, and the chemical companies began to discharge some of their workers. Harold returned to the University of Montana, where he had been offered a position as Instructor of Chemistry. Soon, however, he realized that if he was going to get anywhere as a college teacher, he would have to have a doctor's degree. And he was already twenty-eight years old—an age when many men had already received their Ph.D. degrees. If he was going to go on for further education, he had better get started soon!

In August of 1921, Harold Urey went to Berkeley to enroll in the graduate school of the University of California.

Harold Urey during his stay in Montana, summer 1917 (L) and selling books to Hans "Ole" Tengesdal in the summer of 1921 (R).

Schlechten

# Graduate Studies

In the early 1920's, the University of California was an exciting place for a graduate student in chemistry. The chairman of the department was Professor Gilbert Newton Lewis, who was one of the leaders in the world in the field of physical chemistry. Professor Lewis had a brilliant mind. He came up with a new theory about how atoms, the tiny units of chemical substances, are joined together in chemical bonds. This theory has been changed and built upon since Lewis's time.

Professor Lewis had gathered around him other brilliant teachers, and their students were among the brightest in the country. Many of them went on to start their own physical chemistry departments at other universities, combining a knowledge of physics, chemistry, and mathematics to find out more about the nature of chemical substances and how they react with each other.

Into this exciting graduate school came Harold Urey, and he quickly gained a whole new idea of what a university could be. There were fascinating courses to take, some of them in subjects so new that further discoveries were completely changing them each year. The grade that you got in a course was not important at all—it was what you *learned* that mattered. In fact, Harold was so excited about what he was learning that he never even bothered to go to the Registrar's Office to find out what grades he had received in his courses.

And there was learning to be done outside of the class as well. There were only about thirty graduate students in the chemistry department, and they and the professors all grew to know each other very well. Lively discussions about physical chemistry went on day and night—in the laboratories, in the halls outside the classrooms, and in the dormitories and coffee shops. Every Friday evening there was a seminar, and none of the chemistry graduate students would have missed one of these meetings for anything else. The professors sat around a table in the middle of the room, and the students sat in a circle about them. At the head of the table, Professor Lewis puffed away at a fat cigar. Members of the group gave reports on projects they were working on, and then the discussions bubbled on late into the night.

During this time Urey grew interested in the theories on the structure of the atom. These were the years when the great Danish physicist Niels Bohr and other brilliant scientists were working out the modern ideas of how chemical atoms are put together. Although an individual atom is far too small to see into, even with the best microscopes, scientists had been able to piece together many bits of evidence about how chemical substances behave. Using this evidence, they built up theories of what atoms must be like in order to act as they do.

22

Niels Bohr pictured the atom as a sort of miniature "solar system." The solid bit at the center, called the nucleus, would be like the sun of our solar system. And round about the nucleus, in orbits like those of our sun's planets, travel far tinier particles called electrons.

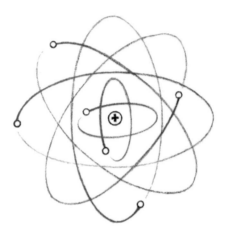

The Bohr atom.

Both the nucleus and the electrons have electric charges. The nucleus has what is called a positive charge, while each electron has a different kind of charge, a negative charge. An atom of any substance has exactly equal amounts of these two different, opposite kinds of electric charges. But sometimes atoms can lose electrons or give them away, or share them with other atoms. This is how chemical reactions occur.

The atoms of different kinds of chemical substances have different numbers of electrons moving about their nuclei. For example, the soot that is formed when a piece of paper is burned is made up mainly of carbon atoms. These atoms each have six electrons. The oxygen and nitrogen in the air we breathe have atoms with eight and seven electrons. Chemists have been able to figure out how many electrons each kind of atom has by studying how chemical substances react with each other. They have also been able to figure out how much the atoms of different substances weigh. And they have found that each kind of atom has its own, definite weight.

For example, a pound of oxygen gas will react with exactly an eighth of a pound of hydrogen gas to form water. A pound of oxygen will react with three-eighths of a pound of carbon to form carbon dioxide, a gas that is found in the used air that we breathe out. For every chemical reaction this sort of weight relationship is observed. Chemists have worked out the weights of each kind of atom and have arranged all the kinds of chemical elements in a series, according to their weight. From this series, a part of which is shown on page 27, it seems that each kind of atom is made up of a certain number of units. A hydrogen atom has one weight unit. An atom of helium, the gas used to fill balloons, has four units. An oxygen atom has sixteen units, while a carbon atom has twelve. There are two kinds of these units: protons, which have a positive charge, and neutrons, which have no charge at all. Both protons and neutrons are found in the nucleus of an atom. (The electrons weigh only $1/1837$ as much as a proton or neutron. Thus their weight makes scarcely any difference at all in the weight of an atom.)

All these theories about the nature of atoms were being worked out at the time that Harold Urey was doing his graduate work. Each year brought exciting new mysteries and exciting new solutions. (In fact, the neutron was not even discovered until 1932.) Chemists were also learning to use mathematics in their work more and more. Mathematical formulas were being developed to describe how atoms are put together and how they behave, and to predict how molecules—groups of atoms joined together—would be constructed.

To earn a Ph.D. degree, a scientist must take a number of courses and learn many facts and theories about his field. But he must also work on a research problem of his own. He must try to make a new discovery in his field of study. Dr. Lewis suggested that Harold Urey work with the metal cesium for his research project. Lewis thought that if this metal were heated up until it turned into a gas, some of the cesium atoms would lose some of their electrons. It was Urey's problem to find out whether this really did happen, and if so, how many of the atoms would lose electrons. It was a difficult problem, and some of the experiments did not work out very well. Then a physicist in India published a fine paper on the very same topic. It was frustrating.

Even though his research project did not work out as well as he had hoped, Harold Urey did learn a great deal about atoms and molecules. The understanding that he gained from this work eventually helped him in the studies that won him a Nobel Prize.

The project also left Urey with a lively interest in astronomy. For stars, such as our sun, are very hot. They are so hot, indeed, that they are great balls of fiery gas. And in such stars, many atoms do lose their electrons.

Astronomers use instruments called spectroscopes and spectrographs to analyze the light that stars send out. These instruments break down the light into a band of colors called a spectrum. When atoms are heated up or when they are ionized (that is, lose electrons), they give out flashes of light energy. Each atom gives out certain types of light, depending on the kind of atom it is, how hot it is, and how many electrons it has

## SOME OF THE CHEMICAL ELEMENTS

| NAME OF ELEMENT | SYMBOL | ATOMIC NUMBER | ATOMIC WEIGHT |
|---|---|---|---|
| Hydrogen | H | 1 | 1.01 |
| Helium | He | 2 | 4.00 |
| Lithium | Li | 3 | 6.94 |
| Beryllium | Be | 4 | 9.01 |
| Boron | B | 5 | 10.81 |
| Carbon | C | 6 | 12.01 |
| Nitrogen | N | 7 | 14.01 |
| Oxygen | O | 8 | 16.00 |
| Fluorine | F | 9 | 19.00 |
| Neon | Ne | 10 | 20.18 |
| Sodium | Na | 11 | 23.00 |
| Magnesium | Mg | 12 | 24.31 |
| Aluminum | Al | 13 | 26.98 |
| Silicon | Si | 14 | 28.09 |
| Phosphorus | P | 15 | 30.97 |
| Sulfur | S | 16 | 32.06 |
| Chlorine | Cl | 17 | 35.45 |
| Argon | Ar | 18 | 39.95 |
| Potassium | K | 19 | 30.10 |
| Calcium | Ca | 20 | 40.08 |
| Iron | Fe | 26 | 55.85 |
| Nickel | Ni | 28 | 58.71 |
| Silver | Ag | 47 | 107.87 |
| Gold | Au | 79 | 196.97 |
| Mercury | Hg | 80 | 200.59 |
| Lead | Pb | 82 | 207.19 |
| Uranium | U | 92 | 238.03 |

lost. And so each atom has its own spectrum, which is different from those of other atoms. By analyzing the light from stars, astronomers can thus tell what kind of atoms they contain, how hot they are, and what kinds of reactions are taking place among them.

In studying cesium atoms, Harold Urey learned how to analyze the light they give off in much the same way. He also studied the spectra of various other gases. He even published a paper about his studies in the *Astronomical Journal.*

In his two years at the University of California, Harold Urey learned and accomplished a great deal. In 1923 he was awarded a Ph.D. degree. Then came another honor. He received a fellowship from the American-Scandinavian Foundation to go to Copenhagen, Denmark, to study with the great Niels Bohr.

# Foreign Travels

The trip to Copenhagen, in August of 1923, was a pleasant one. The American-Scandinavian Foundation had paid Harold Urey's fare on a commercial boat. During the three weeks that it took to cross the Atlantic, he rested, enjoyed the fresh air on deck, and dined with the officers of the boat. In Copenhagen, the Foundation office suggested that the young American scientist might be able to board with Professor Aage Fries, a history professor at the University of Copenhagen. Urey went hopefully to the address he was given, and introduced himself. The Fries family welcomed him with cheerful hospitality; he moved in and soon was made to feel like one of the family.

In the 1920's, Copenhagen was a city of bicycles. Harold quickly bought himself one, and pedaled back and forth each day to the Institute for Theoretical Physics. He also went exploring on weekends through the whole city of Copenhagen. Soon

he grew to love this Danish city. Everything was so clean and orderly, even in the poor sections. There were ancient castles and buildings and statues to gaze at, and wonderful art institutes to visit.

These weekend trips were enjoyable, but Harold Urey's most exciting days were spent at the Institute for Theoretical Physics. Neils Bohr had just been awarded a Nobel Prize for his work on the structure of the atom, and now his little institute was world famous. In addition to Professor Bohr, Georg von Hevesy was working at the institute at the time. (Von Hevesy later won a Nobel Prize for his work on the use of tiny amounts of radioactive substances to study living organisms.) Other famous scientists came to visit from various parts of the world. Among these were two more future Nobel Prize winners, Werner Heisenberg and Wolfgang Pauli. It was thrilling for a young scientist on a fellowship to meet and work with all these brilliant men, and Harold Urey could hardly believe it was happening to him.

During his year at Copenhagen, Urey tried to do some work in theoretical physics. But he soon decided that others, like Heisenberg, Pauli, and even his fellow student John Slater were much better at work in this field than he was. His own strengths in science would lie in other areas. But even as Harold Urey was deciding that he was not cut out to be a theoretical physicist, he was gaining a valuable philosophy. The men at the institute were working on important problems, and making discoveries that brought them world-wide fame. Urey decided that he too would try to seek out important problems, to "hitch his wagon to a star."

The fellowship year at Copenhagen was soon over. Urey took the opportunity to do some traveling in Europe before leaving for home. In Hamburg, Germany, he attended a meeting of the German Physical Society and met two Nobel Prize winners who were later to become life-long friends—Albert Einstein and James Franck. Then he traveled up to Sweden to meet two more Nobel Prize winners, the great chemists Svante Arrhenius and Theodore Svedberg. After brief trips to Paris and London, he finally sailed for the United States on August 15, exactly a year after his arrival in Copenhagen. What a year it had been!

# Marriage and an Important Discovery

Back in America, Harold Urey was faced with a choice: where could he best continue his career in science? He received a National Research Council Fellowship to Harvard University. But Johns Hopkins University in Baltimore, Maryland, offered him a position as a research associate in chemistry, which he decided to accept instead. At Johns Hopkins again he found a stimulating atmosphere. Brilliant men, who later became leaders in their fields, were working at the university. Urey spent hours discussing the latest discoveries in physical chemistry with physicists and chemists. He also attended seminars at the National Bureau of Standards in Washington.

In 1925 Harold Urey took a trip to Seattle, Washington, to visit his mother and stepfather. The ranch in Montana had failed some years before, because the land was poor, and the Longs had moved to Washington. On the way back, Harold decided to stop off at nearby Everett, Washington. Years before, while he was an instructor at the University of Montana, he had become acquainted with a girl named Kate Daum. Now Kate suggested that he might like to meet her younger sister Frieda, who was working as a bacteriologist in a doctor's office in Everett.

As soon as they met, Harold knew immediately that this was the girl he wanted to marry. He stayed on in Everett, and he and Frieda spent the next two weeks hiking in the mountains. Frieda was excited and impressed by the distinguished young research chemist. Harold had so many fascinating stories to tell about the far-off places he had been, the famous people he had met, and the important work he was doing. Harold was delighted to find that Frieda was really interested in his work, and she could understand even the most complicated scientific details. She was lively and attractive, and he was completely in love with her.

Harold wanted to marry Frieda right away and take her back to Baltimore with him. But Frieda was not sure. She had just met Harold, and marriage would be the most important decision of her life. She needed more time to think. That summer Harold Urey and Frieda Daum became engaged, but he had to return to Baltimore without her.

During the following year, while Harold was back at Johns Hopkins, letters flew back and forth as the young couple made plans for the future. In 1926 they were married in Lawrence, Kansas, in Frieda's father's home. Then Frieda joined Harold in Baltimore.

Shortly after his marriage, Harold Urey started on a new project. He and another scientist from the Bureau of Standards in Washington, Arthur Ruark, began to write a book on the

structure of atoms. Ruark was to write the very mathematical parts, while Urey would handle the descriptive chapters.

Work on the book went along very well, although Harold's schedule was upset for awhile when his first child, Gertrude Bessie, was born, in September, 1927. But he soon got used to having a lively baby in the house. By 1929 his work on the book was just about completed.

In 1929 Harold Urey was offered a position as associate professor of chemistry at Columbia University in New York City. He had met some people from Columbia at a scientific meeting, and had a number of interesting discussions with them. Now he decided to go to Columbia to study the spectra of atoms and molecules.

In the fall of 1929, shortly after the birth of his second daughter, Harold Urey took up his new position. A Rowland grating was set up in the Columbia Physics Department. This instrument is a kind of spectrograph that can analyze spectra very precisely. This grating had actually been made at Johns Hopkins University many years before, but it had never been used. Now Harold Urey could use it for his work. This was a wonderful opportunity. Though Johns Hopkins had some excellent gratings, they were being used constantly by a physicist, Professor R. W. Wood. If Harold had stayed in Baltimore, he could not have used these instruments at all.

Soon after Harold Urey began work at Columbia, his attention was distracted by an interesting new problem. A British scientist, Francis Aston, had developed an instrument called a mass spectrograph. This instrument gave a spectrum that was quite different from the spectra formed by the spectroscopes that astronomers use. Each line on the spectrum from a mass spectrograph corresponds to atoms and ions of one particular weight.

Working with his mass spectrograph, Aston began to study gases of various chemical elements and made an important discovery. The atoms of a particular element are not all alike after all. They all react in the same way chemically, but they may have different atomic weights. For example, in the gas neon, which is used to light up neon signs, Aston found lines from two different kinds of atoms. One had an atomic weight of 20, while the other type had a weight of 22. These different varieties of the same chemical element are called isotopes. Now scientists know that the neon isotope with a weight of 20 has ten electrons, ten protons, and ten neutrons. The isotope of neon with a weight of 22 also has ten electrons and ten protons, but it has twelve neutrons in its nucleus. (There is another isotope of neon with an atomic weight of 21—ten electrons, ten protons, and eleven neutrons—but this isotope is present in such minute amounts that Aston did not find it.)

Using his mass spectrograph, Aston compared the hydrogen atom with the oxygen atom, which has an atomic weight of 16, and determined the atomic weight of hydrogen. He got exactly the same value as chemists who had determined the atomic weights of the two elements according to their chemical reactions. Everyone was pleased to see that the results obtained by two different methods checked so well.

But then Professor William Giauque at the University of California discovered that oxygen has three different isotopes, with atomic weights of 16, 17, and 18. Any sample of oxygen contains mostly oxygen-16, but it also has very small amounts of the other two isotopes as well.

Now everyone was confused. The chemists who had determined the atomic weights of oxygen and hydrogen had thought that all their oxygen had a weight of 16. Now that they knew about the other isotopes, they realized they had been working with a mixture whose atomic weight was slightly more than 16. This meant that the weight for hydrogen must be slightly larger, too. But now their results did not check with Aston's results any more. Aston really had been working with pure oxygen-16, for a line on a mass spectrum is formed by atoms all of the same weight.

Professors R. T. Birge and Donald Menzel suggested that hydrogen, too, must have a heavier isotope. From the new weight values, they calculated that there should be one atom of the heavier hydrogen for every five thousand or so of the ordinary kind.

Now the problem was to prove that the heavier isotope of hydrogen really existed. But if it did exist, it was present in such very small amounts! How could it be detected?

Harold Urey had an idea. If he analyzed the spectrum of a sample of hydrogen on a spectrograph, the two isotopes should give different sets of lines. But there was still a problem. The lines of the heavier isotope would be very faint, because there was so little of it in the sample. And instruments are not perfect. Sometimes stray lines appear in a spectrum that are not caused by anything in the sample at all, but just by imperfections in the spectrograph. If Urey did find faint lines that might be due to the new isotope of hydrogen, how could he be really sure that that was what they were? How could he prove that the new lines were not just stray instrument lines? If only there were some way to get a sample of hydrogen that contained *more* of the heavier isotope than usual—if it did exist! Then the new lines would be much stronger.

Harold Urey sat down to think about the problem. If the new theories were correct, the ordinary isotope of hydrogen would have a weight of 1—one proton and one electron. The heavier isotope would have a weight of 2—one proton, one electron, and one neutron. Now that is quite a big difference: the atom of the heavier isotope would actually be twice as heavy as the atom of the ordinary kind. With that large a difference in weights, perhaps the isotopes would behave differently in other ways too.

Urey's work on gases gave him some other ideas, and he began to put them together. If liquid hydrogen were warmed, it would turn into a gas or vapor. But molecules of the lighter isotope should have what is called a higher vapor pressure than those of the heavier isotope. That is, they should be able to move faster and so fly off as a vapor more quickly than the heavier atoms. As a result, there should be relatively fewer atoms of the heavier isotope in the vapor, and more in the liquid that was left behind. If a sample of liquid hydrogen were heated until nearly all of the liquid had evaporated, then the small amount of liquid left behind should have a much larger proportion of the heavier isotope than the original liquid. Urey and his assistant, George Murphy, calculated exactly how great the difference should be.

It seems amazing that scientists could figure out so much about substances that had never been isolated—and indeed that they were not even sure really existed. Yet this is what the powerful methods of physical chemistry have made it possible to do.

Now Harold Urey wrote to an old friend at the National Bureau of Standards in Washington, Ferdinand Brickwedde. He told his friend about his new ideas and asked him to distill some hydrogen, that is, to heat up some liquid hydrogen until it formed a gas. Brickwedde did this and sent the samples to

Urey. Eagerly Urey began to study the new samples on the Rowland grating.

On Thanksgiving day, 1931, the first clear results came in. That evening, when Harold arrived home for dinner, he announced proudly to his wife, "Well, Frieda, I think we've arrived!"

Carefully Harold Urey checked his results. The new lines were definitely there. In fact, he also found them in the spectra of ordinary samples of hydrogen. But, just as he had expected, the lines of the new isotope were much stronger in the concentrated samples that Dr. Brickwedde had sent him.

In December of 1931, Urey announced to the world that a heavier isotope of hydrogen had been discovered. He named it deuterium, from a word meaning "second." For it was the second isotope of hydrogen, and also the second isotope in the series of all the elements arranged by weight.

Later the Rowland grating was taken apart. It seems that the discovery of heavy hydrogen was the only scientific problem for which this instrument was ever used.

# The Nobel Prize

Work on the new isotope, deuterium, did not come to a stop after it had been officially discovered. Indeed, scientists in many laboratories throughout the world were inspired by Harold Urey's announcement to begin their own studies of the isotope. They wanted to see if they could repeat Urey's experiments, to find better methods of obtaining larger amounts of deuterium, and to find out more about it.

The new studies quickly yielded some very curious results. First of all, it was found that Professor Aston had made a mistake. It was one of the few mistakes he had ever made, but the value he had calculated for the atomic weight of hydrogen was wrong. Then it was found that the chemists who had determined the atomic weight of hydrogen had made a mistake, too! The two mistakes had canceled each other out. So the perfectly correct prediction made by Professors Birge and Menzel, which had led to the discovery of deuterium, was actually based on two incorrect reports!

Harold Urey shook his head in wonder when the papers on the new studies were published. He was famous now for discovering deuterium, and none of it would have happened if two other scientists had not made two completely unrelated errors. What a piece of luck!

Meanwhile, Urey was following up some new isotope projects. It had occurred to him that although all the isotopes of a particular element take part in the same kinds of chemical reactions, the heavier isotopes might react more slowly than the lighter ones. He and his associates began to work out a theory of this and developed methods for separating the isotopes of various elements—hydrogen, oxygen, carbon, nitrogen, and sulfur—by chemical reactions.

Urey was also working closely with Dr. Edward Washburn at the Bureau of Standards in Washington. They were trying to work out a method for obtaining pure heavy water. (A molecule of ordinary water contains two atoms of the light isotope of hydrogen and one of oxygen.) Urey and Washburn hoped to get their heavy water by a process called electrolysis. If an electric current is passed through a water solution containing sodium hydroxide, the water is broken down into hydrogen and oxygen gases. Dr. Washburn thought that since the light isotope of hydrogen becomes a gas more easily, this isotope would escape more rapidly in the gas formed in electrolysis. He tried this out and found that he was right. As electrolysis proceeds, and the gases escape, the water that is left behind becomes richer and richer in the deuterium form. If the process is repeated over and over again, eventually only heavy water is left.

The heavy water project went very slowly, because Urey and Washburn did not have enough supplies and equipment to work with. But back at the University of California, Gilbert Lewis, Harold Urey's old professor, was also working on the same problem. Lewis was the chairman of one of the most important chemistry departments in the country, and he had all the money and equipment he needed. And so in 1933 it was Gilbert Lewis who announced that the first sample of pure heavy water had been obtained. Urey felt a little hurt at this. In future years, whenever one of his students made an important discovery, he tried to help the student as much as possible, rather than to take the subject away from him.

Harold Urey swallowed his disappointment at losing the heavy-water race and worked on. He and his research group got some good results on the chemical separation of isotopes, and in 1934 he was promoted to full professor. He tried to spend more time with his family, too. Gertrude Bessie had grown into a spirited little imp, who had recently announced that she was planning to change her name to Elizabeth. The second daughter, Frieda Rebecca, was a sturdy little girl too. It seemed to their proud father that both children were unusually bright. They certainly were lively. Frieda Urey had her hands full, especially since she was now expecting another child.

One November afternoon in 1934, Harold Urey was at lunch at the Faculty Club when he was called to the telephone. It was a newspaper reporter, who informed Urey that he had just received the Nobel Prize in Chemistry for 1934. Harold was dazed. A friend of his, Professor Enric Zanetti, had been insisting that Harold would be elected, but Harold had not thought it at all likely. Now he didn't know whether to believe the reporter or not. After all, he had not received any telegram from the Swedish Academy of Sciences. Perhaps it was all a mistake.

With a start, Harold realized that he was still holding the telephone receiver in his hand. He dialed his home number to tell Frieda about the news. But the line was busy. In fact, it was busy all afternoon, every time he tried to call home.

At last, at about four o'clock, a telegram arrived from Stockholm. It was official now. Harold Urey had been awarded a Nobel Prize.

Now Harold Urey had a difficult decision to make. He was invited to Stockholm for the Nobel Prize festivities. He would receive his prize from the hands of the King of Sweden himself, and then he would deliver an acceptance speech before all the assembled scientists and nobles. The actual prize-giving would start on December 10, and before that there would be a gay round of sightseeing and parties and formal dinners. But Frieda was due to have her baby early in December. How could he leave her now?

Finally Harold decided to stay with his wife, and he was with her when their third daughter, Mary Alice, was born on December 2, 1934. Together they read the newspaper accounts of the Nobel Prize awards taking place across the sea.

"You should have been there," said Frieda with a guilty sigh.

"Don't worry," Harold laughed. "They'll save it for us."

In February Harold and Frieda Urey left the children with friends, Professor and Mrs. Ray Christ, and sailed to Stockholm. There Harold received the Nobel Prize, a gold medal and a cash award of $41,000. He gazed at the medal in wonder. "I'm a Nobel Prize winner!" he thought. He had known many Nobel Prize winners—Langmuir, Franck, Einstein—how could he possibly live up to the reputation of men like those? Well, there was nothing to do but go on working and do the best he could.

# The War Years

The years after the Nobel Prize award were happy ones for the Ureys. They used part of the prize money to build a lovely house in Leonia, New Jersey. Harold continued his work at Columbia University on the separation of isotopes, aided by a group of bright young graduate students.

But as Harold watched the news from Europe, he grew more and more troubled. Hitler had come to power and was building up Germany's military forces. Einstein, Franck, and other prominent scientists were fleeing from the Nazis and taking up new lives in America.

"There's a war coming," Urey told his friends, "a full-scale war." But there were not many who believed him.

Late in the summer of 1939, Frieda Urey gave birth to a son, John Clayton. Two days later Hitler invaded Poland, and World War II began.

In the late 1930's some important scientific discoveries had been made, which were ultimately to involve Harold Urey in war work again. It had been discovered that if an atom of the element uranium is hit with a neutron, it will split apart, just as a soft rock will split into pieces if you hit it with a hammer. The pieces that break off from the uranium atom are nuclei of lighter elements, and in addition, large amounts of energy are released. More neutrons are also produced, and they can go on to hit other uranium atoms and cause them to split too. These splitting reactions are called nuclear fission.

Uranium, like the other elements, is a mixture of isotopes. As the fission reactions were studied, it was found that they worked best with the isotope uranium-235. But this is a rather rare isotope; any sample of uranium contains much more of another isotope, uranium-238. It was clear that if fission reactions were going to be put to any practical use, a way to separate the isotopes would have to be found.

Of course Harold Urey was interested in the new problem, since he had been working on the separation of isotopes for some time. But he knew that the kind of chemical separations he had been using would not be good for uranium. For chemical separations work best for very light elements, and uranium atoms are the heaviest of all those found in nature. Some other way would have to be found.

A physicist at Columbia University, Professor John Dunning, thought that the uranium isotopes could be separated by a process called diffusion. You can see for yourself how diffusion works by placing a drop of vegetable dye in a glass of water. At first the drop of dye is all in one spot. But gradually the color spreads through the water. If you leave the glass alone long enough, the dye will color all of the water.

The molecules of vegetable dye, just like the molecules of everything else, are constantly in motion. If nothing stops them, they will eventually spread all through the container in which they are placed. This is diffusion.

Harold Urey had a different idea. He was working with another physicist, Jesse Beams, at separating atoms on a high-speed centrifuge. This is an instrument in which substances in long tubes are spun around. The heaviest substances move to the outside of the rotating cylinder, while the lighter ones concentrate toward the center.

Later it was found that it would also be useful to separate some isotopes of lighter elements, such as hydrogen and boron. For these isotopes, chemical methods would be useful, and Urey was asked to serve on a committee to study ways of separating them.

Work on the fission project went very slowly at first. But then Leo Szilard and other physicists persuaded Albert Einstein to write a letter to President Roosevelt to tell him how important the project really was. In 1940 a nuclear energy project was organized under the leadership of Vannevar Bush. Later the project was taken over by the army, under General Leslie R. Groves, and groups were set up at Columbia University, the University of Chicago, and the University of California to work on various problems involved in building an atomic bomb.

Harold Urey was asked to head the team working at Columbia. He was shocked and dismayed. He tried to persuade General Groves's assistant, Colonel Nichols, that John Dunning was really the man who should head the project. After all, it was Dunning who had been working steadily on the separation of uranium isotopes, and this physicist was a very able organizer and administrator, too. But Colonel Nichols refused to listen,

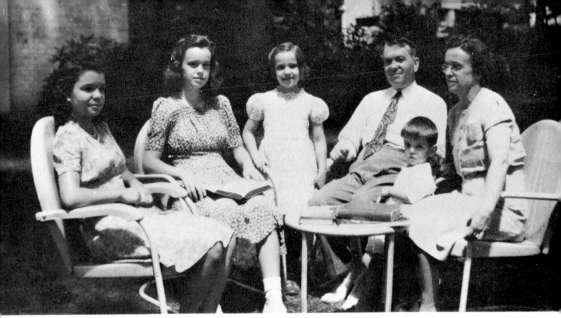

The Urey family at home in Leonia, New Jersey, in 1942.

and Urey felt forced to accept the position of director of the Substitute Alloy Materials Laboratory at Columbia.

Years later it occurred to Urey that the government probably had very little faith that the atom bomb project would ever succeed, and they wanted a Nobel Prize winner around to take the blame if it failed. He had made a mistake in accepting the position. He should have tried harder to refuse, or perhaps gone to Dunning to talk things over. But by the time he realized all this it was too late.

The war years were very troubling and discouraging ones for Harold Urey. Not only was he working on a project that might some day be used to destroy the lives of millions of people, but the work was not even going well. He was the director, responsible for the work of many men and women, and he was more and more becoming convinced that he just was not made to be an administrator at all. He had trouble remembering details of organization, even while he could recall the most minute scientific facts with the greatest ease. Dunning's group was unhappy because they would have preferred to have John Dunning as their director, and so they had trouble cooperating with the others working on the project. Problems kept coming up, and Urey became so discouraged about their ever being solved that he was close to becoming physically ill. And on top of everything else, all the work had to be done under the strictest secrecy. Urey was not even supposed to tell his wife what he was doing.

At last, in February of 1945, the ordeal was over. Harold Urey was removed from his position and a new director was appointed. He was enormously relieved and completely exhausted. It took a full month of just resting before he was able to work again, even on the simplest sort of scientific problems. In 1946, after the war was over, Urey and Dunning received the Medal of Merit for their work on the project.

General Leslie Groves pins the Medal for Merit on Harold Urey, 1946.

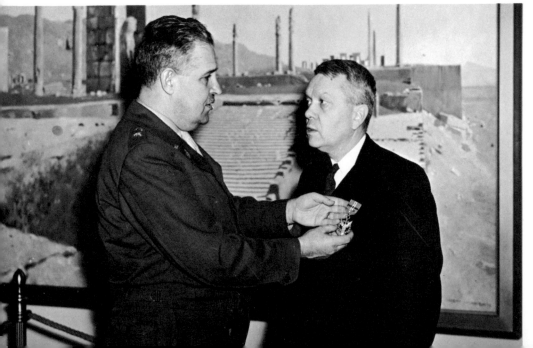

# New Interests

At the end of the war, the Ureys had the feeling that it was time for another change. The isotope separation project had left Harold with many unhappy memories of the group at Columbia. He was also getting rather bored with the job of separating isotopes, which he had been doing for more than a dozen years.

Now Harold Urey was interested to hear that a new institute was being planned at the University of Chicago. Such famous scientists as Enrico Fermi, Willard Libby, and James Franck would be working at the institute. So Urey decided to move to Chicago.

Soon Harold and Frieda Urey and their four lively children were settled in a big old house in the south part of Chicago. Harold found the university a wonderfully stimulating place. For a while he drifted from one project to another, unable to find work that really interested him. He tried working on the use of isotopes in problems in chemistry. But then he discovered that he had a sort of mental block. He did not want to use any radioactive isotopes, even when they would be the best tools for the job. "This is foolish," he thought. But try as he would, he just could not seem to get interested in problems involving radioactive isotopes. Perhaps it would be best to find an entirely new problem to work on.

An interesting new problem did come up. During his studies in the thirties, Urey had shown that different isotopes of an element have slightly different chemical properties. He had used these differences to separate isotopes. Now it occurred to him that chemical reactions go on all the time in living organisms. These reactions depend to some degree on the temperature. If Urey determined the amounts of various isotopes in fossils of ancient sea creatures, he ought to be able to figure out the temperatures of the oceans in which they lived. And in this way he would work out a temperature history for the earth's oceans.

Now Harold Urey began to study samples of calcium carbonate rocks, which had been formed from the shells of sea animals that lived long ages ago. He found just the sort of relationship that he had expected. The more of the heavy isotope oxygen-18 in the rocks, the colder the water in which they were formed. With a group of students, including Cesare Emiliani and Harmon Craig, who are still actively working in the field, Urey began work on a fossil of a very interesting creature. It was a squid-like animal, called a cephalopod. This creature formed a calcium carbonate skeleton that contained growth rings, very much like the rings that can be seen in the cut stump of a tree trunk. Urey and his students carved off each growth ring very carefully and studied each sample separately. They

54

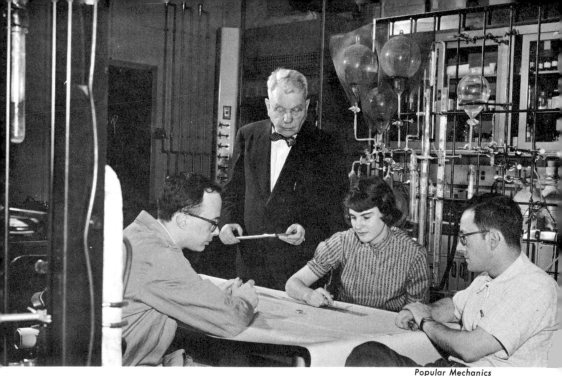

Popular Mechanics

Harold Urey at the University of Chicago with Professor Cesare Emiliani, Professor Gerald Wasserburg, and a student.

discovered that the temperature had varied back and forth during the animal's life. In fact, it was quite easy to tell which part of a ring had been formed in the winter and which part in the summer. From their tests of the last growth ring, they decided that the cephalopod had died some time in the spring, perhaps in April or May. It amused the scientists to realize that although they had just figured out what month the cephalopod had died in, this creature had lived its life about sixty *million* years before the names of the months were invented!

Working on this new project, Harold Urey grew interested in geology. He had taken a course in the subject in college, but he had found it boring to look at collections of different kinds of rocks. Now he was actively studying the history of life forms on the earth, and he began to read all the geology books he could find. He found a popular book on the subject and read it to his small son John. As Harold taught the names of the geological periods to his son, he also learned them himself.

Urey went on with his isotope studies and found that at various times in the past history of the earth, the climates have been quite different from those we have now. For example, about a hundred million years ago, the oceans near Europe were much warmer than they are now.

Urey found his studies of the temperatures of the ancient earth very interesting. But after a time he began to realize that there was a limit to how far he could go in this field. He had been trained as a physical chemist, not a geologist. Although he had gained a great deal of knowledge in geology since he had become interested in the field, he was still constantly amazed at how much more the real geological experts knew. On a collecting trip with Heinz Lowenstamm in the southern United States, Harold found that his friend could tell just by looking at a rock how old it was, while he often could not tell what was important and what was not.

At last Urey decided to leave the field of determining past temperatures to the men he had trained, such as Emiliani, Craig, and Lowenstamm. For now he was becoming intrigued by a new problem.

One of Urey's colleagues, Harrison Brown, had been studying meteorites, pieces of matter that have fallen to earth from the sky. Urey did not want to intrude on someone else's subject. But then Harrison Brown left the University of Chicago and went to work at the California Institute of Technology. Now Urey felt free to follow up his growing interest in meteorites.

At the same time, a book called *Face of the Moon,* by Ralph Baldwin, was published, and the publisher sent a free copy to Urey. Glancing into the book, Urey became interested and read it through. He also received some photographs of the moon from the Harvard University astronomer Harlow Shapley. He pasted these pictures together to make a giant map of the moon, about three feet across. Gazing at the map, Urey began to wonder what had caused all the craters and other landmarks on the face of the moon. It seemed to him that something must have

Harold Urey with the giant map of the moon that first sparked his interest in the moon's history.

struck the moon in a great collision to form one of the great "seas" or maria. Then there were smaller collisions, forming craters of various sizes, which partly covered the mare. He thought that these collisions must have occurred very long ago, perhaps while the earth itself was being formed. And so the rocks of the moon might hold the story of the early history of our own planet too. On earth that record has been covered up by the great changes that have occurred here over the past few billion years.

Urey began to study the chemistry of rocks and meteorites, and to try to piece together a story of how the earth, the moon, and the planets were formed. He wrote a book about his studies and readings, called *The Planets, Their Origin and Development.* The book was a great success in the scientific world, and Urey soon met many astronomers and geologists. Some of them gave him great honors, but some seemed unfriendly somehow, as though they felt he should have stayed in his own field and not come butting into theirs.

Harold Urey's studies on the origin of the planets led him to wonder again about how life began on earth. From studies of the spectra of stars and rocks on the earth, it seemed to him that the ancient earth must have been very different from the one we know now. The air we breathe now consists mainly of two gases—about four parts nitrogen to one part of oxygen. But before life began, Urey thought, there was probably no oxygen in the air at all. Instead, the atmosphere probably contained large amounts of hydrogen, methane, and ammonia. Life as we know it could not thrive in such an atmosphere. But the first life could have formed there. For ultraviolet rays from the sun streamed down upon the ancient earth, and its atmosphere was cut again and again by crackling flashes of lightning. With all this energy striking the gas molecules of the atmosphere, they could easily combine to form more complicated chemicals. And, given enough time, these complicated chemicals could develop into life.

Urey wrote a paper about these ideas, and in 1952 he gave a speech on the origin of life at a seminar in the chemistry department. When he returned to his office after the seminar, he found a young graduate student, Stanley Miller, waiting for him. Miller said that he had been fascinated by the speech, and he wanted to work on the problem for his Ph.D. project. Harold Urey practically never tried to discourage a student who wanted to work on a particular project. But this time he tried. He honestly did not think that this was the sort of problem that could be worked out in the laboratory, and he told Miller so.

But Stanley Miller refused to be discouraged. He was determined to work on the problem. Finally Urey shrugged, "Well, let's go ahead." And he and Stanley Miller spent the next few days discussing what they could do to re-create conditions like those of the ancient earth. They decided to mix methane, ammonia, water, and hydrogen, send an electric spark through the mixture, and see what happened.

Miller went off to plan his apparatus and set up the experiment. When everything was ready, he ran the experiment for about a week and then carefully separated the substances that were dissolved in the water. He found amino acids, which are the building blocks of proteins, one of the most important kinds of chemicals of life. A report on this experiment was published in May 1953. Miller ran further careful studies and then wrote up his doctoral dissertation. It was very well received, and he was awarded a Ph.D. degree in 1954.

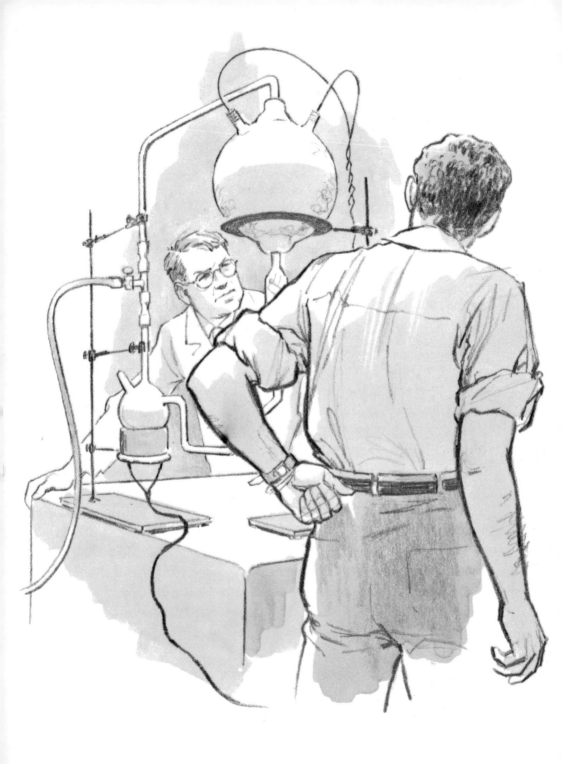

Miller and Urey published reports about the experiments, and the scientific world was thrilled. This was the first time that anyone had reproduced the conditions of the ancient earth in the laboratory and shown how chemicals of life could have been formed. Other researchers repeated the experiments again and again. They tried variations, adding other simple chemicals or bits of rock, and they obtained a whole variety of chemicals of life. Gradually they built up a picture of how life was formed on earth.

# Another Change

In 1956 Harold Urey received an invitation to be Visiting Professor at Oxford University in England. He spent a pleasant year there, lecturing about his theories on how life began on earth and on the origin of the solar system. But then, after a short time back in Chicago, Harold and Frieda began to feel that they would like to make another change.

"I guess we are rolling stones," says Urey. "Some people spend their whole life at one university. I have wandered many places, partly from necessity, but mostly by choice."

In 1958 Urey became sixty-five years old and thus eligible to retire from the University of Chicago. He began to make plans. But these were not plans for a quiet retirement in the country, puttering about on his hobbies. He was thinking about taking a new job.

Not long before, a man named Roger Revelle had come to

Chicago and had been introduced to Harold Urey. He told Urey about a new college that was being organized at San Diego, as a part of the University of California. The new college would be associated with the Scripps Institution of Oceanography, and this intrigued Harold very much. For he had always been interested in biology, and he had already done a great deal of work on determining the temperatures of the oceans long ago. He grew even more excited when he realized that some old friends of his would also be there—Harmon Craig, to whom he had taught the methods of studying ocean temperatures using isotopes, and Hans Suess, with whom he had written a paper on the relative abundances of the chemical elements.

So at the age of sixty-five, Harold Urey became a Professor at Large at the University of California in San Diego. He and

Dr. Urey at University of California Irvine Lecture, 1967.

Frieda bought a house in La Jolla, California, with a beautiful garden in the back. Friends gave them some orchids, and soon Harold became fascinated with the hobby of raising these lovely flowers. The patio of the little house is now a burst of color, filled with many varieties of orchids. There is also a little orchid house, in which the more delicate ones are kept.

Frieda Urey in the garden at La Jolla, California.

The Urey children are all grown by now, and they have given Harold and Frieda much pleasure and pride.

Elizabeth, the oldest, married a young physicist, Michel Baranger. They now live in Lexington, Massachusetts, where Michel is a Professor of Physics at Massachusetts Institute of Technology. Elizabeth cares for their three children and still finds time to work as a Senior Scientist at the Institute. Recently

Harold and Frieda proudly attended a meeting of the American Physical Society in Washington, where their daughter presented a lecture on the structure of certain atoms.

Frieda Rebecca earned a doctor's degree, and she too began a scientific career. But after her marriage to a lawyer, Joseph Brown, she decided to give up her career until she has finished raising her family. Now she and her husband, with their two bright young children, live in Cleveland, Ohio.

Mary Alice earned a master's degree at the University of Chicago and then taught in grade schools for a time. Now she and her husband, Emmett Bernard Lorey, who is a physician, live in Palo Alto, California, with their three children.

The fourth Urey, John Clayton, is also a scientist. He married a grandniece of his father's old friend, Irving Langmuir. After completing research at the University of California in Los Angeles, John moved on, with his wife Ann and small son, to Massachusetts, where he holds a position at Wheaton College.

Harold Urey has not had as much time to visit with his growing family and enjoy his orchids as he might have liked. For not long after he returned from the University of Oxford, he was plunged into a new activity. In 1958 he was invited to be a member of a committee to consider what should be done about the United States space program. And ever since then he has been busy with plans and studies connected with the exploration of the moon.

Dr. Urey thinks of the space program as a great adventure and is proud to have been a part of the effort that put the first men on the moon. Ever since he became associated with the program, he has been eagerly studying what is known about the moon and trying to bring his own ideas on the subject up to date. For a while he had some troubles. It seemed to Urey that the surface of the moon, as we see it now, is a very ancient surface, formed billions of years ago. He believed, too, that the great craters on the face of the moon were caused by enormous collisions, and that any volcanos on the moon must be very small. Many other scientists did not believe that these ideas were correct at all. They thought that changes such as great volcanic explosions have been occurring on the moon's surface quite recently, and thus the surface of the moon is very young. At scientific meetings and conferences, Urey constantly had to defend his ideas over and over again. This made him quite unhappy. For there was really no way to *prove* who was right until men actually went to the moon and brought back samples of its rocks.

Now that has been done at last. As the Apollo 11 astronauts left on their mission to the moon, in July, 1969, Harold Urey waited anxiously, hoping that they would land and return safely. He was eager to see what they would bring back with them. A local newspaper had an editorial on the moon mission, ending with the words, "and may God go with them." When he read these words, Urey added, "and may the Mission Control Center and the computers go with them too."

When the astronauts returned with their samples of moon rocks, Harold Urey was even busier than ever. He was working at the Lunar Receiving Laboratory in Houston, and flying about the country to meetings with other scientists examining the new samples. Reports began to come in, and in January, 1970, a week-long conference was held in Houston to discuss what the scientists had found. And it seems that Harold Urey was right after all.

Various samples of moon rock were found to be three and a half billion years old and the soil even four and a half billion

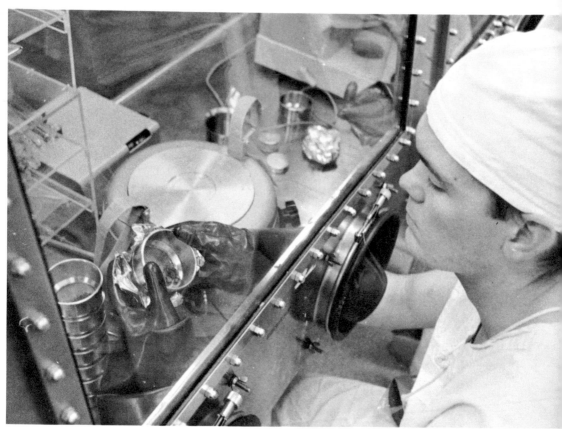

A NASA scientist examines an Apollo 11 moon rock sample inside a special air-tight, germ-free chamber at the Lunar Receiving Laboratory in Houston.

years old. Samples of glassy substances showed that there had been enormous explosions on the surface of the moon, so great that the rocks melted and huge craters were formed. Scientists are not yet sure whether these explosions were caused by collisions or by the eruption of huge volcanos. But whatever caused them, they all occurred long, long ago. It seems that the surface of the moon has been relatively quiet for more than three and a half billion years.

The rocks of the moon were also found to contain much less oxygen than the rocks of the earth. And this finding, too, gives support to Harold Urey's ideas about the origin of life on earth. For he, and other scientists in the field, believe that when the earth was young there was no free oxygen in the air—not until living organisms began to live and grow and then began to release oxygen as part of their life activities. Only then could oxygen from the air have joined with the rocks of the earth's surface. If the moon truly was formed at about the same time as the earth and in about the same way—and this is what the samples of moon rocks seem to show—then explorers of the moon will be bringing back rock records to show how our own planet developed in the earliest days, before life appeared. And this is exactly what Harold Urey had hoped and dreamed.

A close-up view of an Apollo 12 moon rock sample collected by Astronaut Alan Bean in a small crater.

National Aeronautics and Space Administration

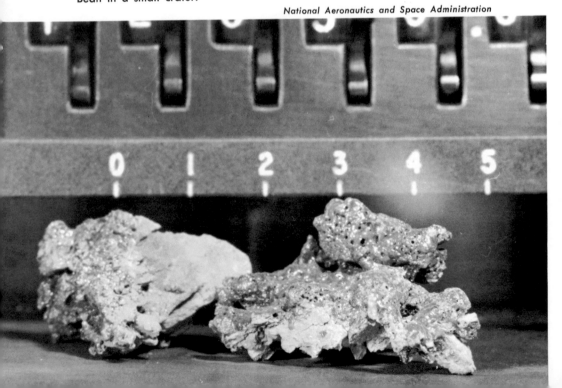

# A Life of Growing

The life story of Harold Clayton Urey has been one of constant growth. His parents believed that a good education is the best preparation for contributing something worthwhile to society. Harold Urey firmly believes this, too. "The social problems in the United States today," he says, "are not just going to go away. All the people—American Indians, Blacks, Mexicans, Chinese, Japanese, or any other—are eventually going to be brought into this society by one method or another. And we had better try our best to make all our people the best kind of people we possibly can. It is my belief that we should invest heavily in food for pregnant mothers and their children. We should invest in Headstart, kindergartens, elementary and high schools, trade schools, colleges, universities—all kinds of schools; for education is our best hope."

Harold Urey's own life is a shining example of his philosophy. Because he has always been eager to learn and grow, he has been able to do important work not just in one field, but in many—chemistry, physics, biology, geology, and astronomy. His Nobel Prize was won for the discovery of deuterium. This discovery has had many far-reaching results. Deuterium has turned out to be an important part of the hydrogen bomb, and this application has made Harold Urey very sad. But deuterium also holds great promise for providing sources of cheap electrical power for the world through peaceful uses of nuclear energy. And its discoverer is very pleased that it should be of use in this way.

Dr. and Mrs. Urey look at a commemorative plaque at the dedication of Harold C. Urey Hall at Revelle College, California, May 1966.

Glasheen Graphics

Urey's studies using isotopes to determine the temperatures of the ancient seas led to the use of isotopes in a great variety of problems in geology. These studies have done much to increase man's knowledge of his world and its past history.

Urey's ideas on the origin of life on earth inspired his student, Stanley Miller, to conduct the first successful laboratory experiments in this fields. Since then, many other scientists have become interested in studies of how life began on earth, and each year they are gaining a clearer picture of the far distant history of our planet.

And now, Harold Urey is at the forefront of one of man's most exciting adventures—exploring worlds beyond the earth. He has helped in the study of moon rocks, and he is looking ahead to the first missions to Mars.

Great scientists have won world fame for a single important discovery in a whole lifetime. But the work and discoveries of Harold Clayton Urey have spanned many fields and have opened up new horizons for mankind.

# Important Events
## in the Life of Harold Urey

1893    Born in Walkerton, Indiana, on April 29.

1911    Finishes high school; qualifies as schoolteacher.

1917    Receives BS degree from University of Montana; becomes a chemist after United States enters World War I.

1919    Becomes Instructor of Chemistry at University of Montana.

1923    Receives Ph.D. degree from University of California and fellowship to study with Niels Bohr at Institute of Theoretical Physics in Copenhagen, Denmark.

1924    Becomes Research Associate in Chemistry at Johns Hopkins University.

1926   Marries Frieda Daum.

1927   Daughter Gertrude Bessie (Elizabeth) is born.

1929   Becomes Associate Professor of Chemistry at Columbia University; daughter Frieda Rebecca is born.

1930   Publishes *Atoms, Molecules, and Quanta* with A. E. Ruark.

1931   Discovers deuterium.

1934   Promoted to Full Professor; awarded Nobel Prize in Chemistry; daughter Mary Alice is born.

Harold Urey in his office at Revelle College, 1967.

1939   Son John Clayton is born; World War II is declared.

1940   Appointed director of Substitute Alloy Materials Laboratory at Columbia in nuclear energy project.

1946   Receives Medal of Merit for work on nuclear energy project; takes position at University of Chicago; begins work on isotope determination of temperatures of ancient seas.

1952   Publishes *The Planets, Their Origin and Development*.

1953   Publishes first report on origin of life experiments with Stanley Miller.

1956   George Eastman Visiting Professor at Oxford University.

1958   Retires from University of Chicago; becomes Professor at Large at Revelle College of University of California at San Diego.

1959   Joins committee on United States space program.

1969   Apollo 11 astronauts land on the moon and bring back samples confirming Urey's theory that surface of moon dates from early history of solar system.

# Glossary

AMINO ACID—A chemical consisting of carbon, hydrogen, oxygen, and nitrogen (and sometimes sulfur) with an amino group (-NH₂) at one end and an acid group ( -COOH) at the other. There are about twenty kinds of amino acids in living things.

ATOM—The tiniest unit of a chemical element that still has all the characteristics of that element.

CELL—The basic unit of life. Some organisms consist of a single cell; our bodies contain trillions of cells of many different types, all working together.

CHEMICAL REACTION—A process in which chemical elements or compounds break down or join together or exchange atoms or groups of atoms, forming new substances.

DEUTERIUM—An isotope of hydrogen which contains one proton, one electron, and one neutron. (The most common isotope of hydrogen contains one proton, one electron, and no neutrons.)

75

DISTILLATION—The heating of a liquid until it becomes a gas, followed by cooling to change the gas back into a liquid. Distillation is often used to separate mixtures of liquids that boil at different temperatures.

ELECTROLYSIS—The passage of an electric current through a liquid, causing a chemical reaction.

ELECTRON—A particle within an atom, which possesses a negative electric charge. The electrons of an atom are found outside the nucleus and are much smaller than the protons and neutrons.

HEAVY WATER—Water containing deuterium and oxygen instead of normal hydrogen and oxygen.

HYDROGEN—The lightest and simplest of all the elements.

ION—An electrically charged atom or group of atoms.

IONIZATION—A process in which an electrically neutral atom or compound becomes electrically charged by gaining or losing electrons.

ISOTOPES—Varieties of the same element possessing the same numbers of protons and electrons but different numbers of neutrons in each atom.

MARE (pl. MARIA)—A large darkened area on the surface of the moon.

METEORITE—A rock or other piece of matter that has traveled through space and fallen to the ground through the earth's atmosphere.

MOLECULE—A combination of two or more atoms joined together by chemical bonds, formed by the giving or sharing of electrons.

NEUTRON—A particle within an atom, which does not possess an electric charge.

NUCLEUS—The central portion. The nucleus of an atom contains the protons and neutrons.

PROTEIN—A type of chemical found in living things, made up of a long chain of amino acids.

PROTON—A particle within an atom, which possesses a positive electric charge.

PROTOZOA—Microscopic animal-like organisms, composed of a single cell.

RADIOACTIVITY—A tendency of atoms of an element to break down, sending out rays from the nucleus.

SOLAR SYSTEM—A family of planets circling about a central star. Our solar system contains nine planets circling around the sun.

SPECTRUM—A band of colors or a series of bands and lines into which light is broken down by instruments such as spectrographs and spectroscopes.

# Index

# About the Authors

The husband-and-wife team of Alvin Silverstein and Virginia Silverstein have previously written fourteen other books on science for young readers. Dr. Silverstein has been, since 1959, on the faculty of Staten Island Community College of the City University of New York, where he organized a biology program and where he is now a professor. Mrs. Silverstein is a free-lance translator of Russian scientific literature and has worked as an analytical chemist. The Silversteins, who have six young children, live in Brooklyn, New York.